First published in this format 2015

Text and Photos: Vera Vandenbosch
Jacket/Interior Design: Kimberly Adis
Executive Editor, Series: Shawna Mullen
Associate Editor, Series: Timothy Stobierski
Series Art Director: Rosalind Loeb Wanke
Series Production Editor: Lynne Phillips
Copy Editor: Candace B. Levy

The Taunton Press
Inspiration for hands-on living®

The Taunton Press, Inc., 63 South Main Street,
PO Box 5506, Newtown, CT 06470-5506
e-mail: tp@taunton.com

Threads® is a trademark of The Taunton Press, Inc.,
registered in the U.S. Patent and Trademark Office.

The following names/manufacturers appearing in
Friendship Bracelets are trademarks: Herrschners®,
Hobby Lobby®, Jo-Ann Stores℠, LUREX®,
Michaels®

Library of Congress Cataloging-in-Publication Data
Vandenbosch, Vera.
  Friendship bracelets : 12 jewelry designs to make
and share / Vera Vandenbosch.
      pages cm
  Summary: "Friendship Bracelets is a 32-page craft
project booklet containing step-by-step instruction
for making 12 friendship bracelet projects. The
booklet features a Basics section, plus 12 projects,
each accompanied by detailed step-by-step
instructions and step-by-step images."-- Provided by
publisher.
  ISBN 978-1-63186-158-1
1. Friendship bracelets. 2. Silk thread. 3. Slings and
hitches. I. Title.
  TT880.V325 2015
  745.594'2--dc23
                          2014050011

Printed in the United States of America
10 9 8 7 6 5 4 3 2 1

Contents

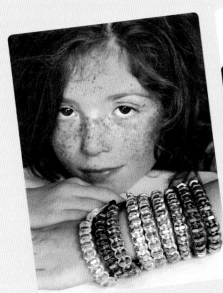

Basic Loom Techniques

Summer camp-style friendship bracelets are all the rage. Typically made with colorful yarn, embroidery floss, or craft cord, they're quick and easy to whip up and look best when worn in multiples. Mix them with other pieces of arm candy, in your own signature color combinations. More is more! Make them for yourself and your friends, trade them or sell them for fundraising or profit. Once you've mastered the basic techniques, it will be easy to move on to other jewelry items: necklaces, earrings, pins . . . you name it.

Six of the projects in this booklet feature a spinning loom, but most everything can be made without the loom with a little ingenuity, so grab some embroidery floss in your favorite colors and get started!

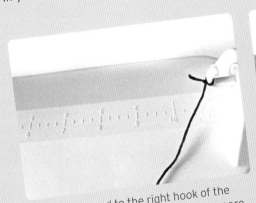

1. Tie the thread to the right hook of the loom with a double knot. You can use more than one thread at the same time.

2. Loosely wrap the thread back and forth around the left and the right hook until you have the core thickness you want. Make sure to end at the left hook.

3. Wrap thread over the core to the front, under to the back, and back to the front, as shown.

4. Tighten, making sure the knot falls at the desired attachment loop width.

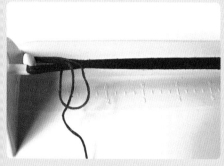

5. Pass the thread from underneath through the attachment loop you just created and back to the front, as shown.

6. Tighten again. The loom is now threaded.

7. Hold the looping thread with your left hand while turning the loom's knob with your right hand away from you.

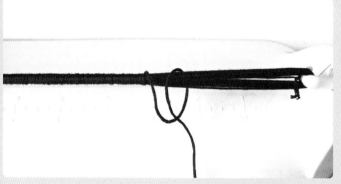

8. When you reach the desired length, make an loop knot as shown.

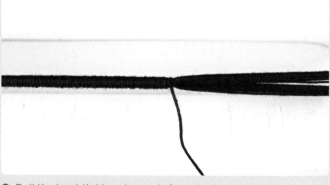

9. Pull the knot tight and repeat (for a double-loop knot).

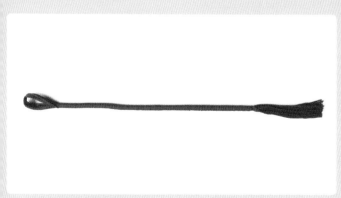

10. Cut the threads close to the right hook and remove the project from the loom. Split the ends in 2 groups and tie a single knot.

11. Tie on your finished bracelet by putting half of the thread through the attachment loop and tying a tight double knot.

Multiple Swirl Bracelet

The easy multicolored twist technique will make your bracelets even faster to create. Group several of these into a sturdy bracelet clasp to showcase all your favorite color combinations!

SKILL LEVEL
Beginner

CORD
Eight 5-yard pieces of embroidery floss in different colors

NOTIONS
Scissors

Spinning loom

Bracelet clasp (1¼ in. by ½ in. or large enough to accommodate 4 bracelets)

Glue of your choice

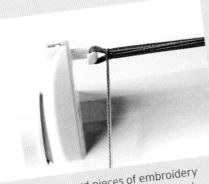

1. Cut eight 5-yard pieces of embroidery thread and sort into 4 groups, with each group having two colors of thread. Take your first set and double knot both colors to the right hook of the spinning loom. Wrap 11 lengths of both threads around the hooks and create an attachment loop ½ in. long on the left side of the loom.

2. Start spinning both threads at the same time, making sure you hold them close to the loom.

3. When your bracelet is 6½ in. long, end with a double-loop knot and cut the threads close to the right hook.

4. Repeat Steps 1 to 3 to make 3 more bracelets. Cut off the remaining threads of all 4 bracelets and insert them into both ends of the bracelet clasp with a few drops of strong glue. Let dry for at least 2 hours before wearing.

Tip

The swirl technique can be used with up to 4 threads with a thicker core. Just make sure to neatly separate the looping threads before you start spinning and hold them between your fingers close to the loom, so that they don't accidentally overlap.

Fishtail Braid Bracelet

The fishtail braid is the hot new hairstyle, so why not use it in your craft projects as well? It does not take long to master and looks great in bright colors, combined with a simple high-gloss wooden bead.

SKILL LEVEL
Beginner

CORD
2 yards of 2 mm satin nylon cord (rattail) in Color A for the base

2 yards of 2 mm satin nylon cord (rattail) in Color B for braiding

NOTIONS
Scissors

Wooden bead, large enough to accommodate 6 strands of nylon cord

Push pin

Foamcore or corkboard

Clear tape of your choice

Thick sewing needle with blunt point

Tip

The trick for making a good-looking fishtail braid is to push the braiding up every once in a while, so the braid remains tight and neat.

1. Decide which color nylon cord to use for the base; this Color A will be visible only at the ends of the bracelet. I used orange for my bracelet. Cut this piece in half. Gather up both lengths of this cord and fold both pieces in half. Make a single knot about 1 in. from the end. This loop should be large enough to slip over the wooden bead. Secure to the foamcore with a push pin. Place the 4 strands of the base neatly next to each other. Fold over the Color B nylon cord to find the middle and place this middle behind the base cord. For my braiding cord, I used blue. Fold both sides over to the front and under the 2 opposite cords, as shown.

2. Fold the strand on the right over to the front, down the middle, and under the left 2 base strands, as shown. Now take the top left strand, fold it over the first 2 strands, down the middle, and under the next 2 strands.

3. Keep braiding until you reach a length of about 6¼ in. Finish with a single firm knot. Turn the braid over and make another single firm knot on the other side of the braid. Cut the ends off at about ¾ in. from the end of the bracelet.

4. Slip all 4 base cords through the bead. If this is tricky, it helps to wrap a piece of clear tape tightly around the cords first. Make a single knot right after the bead. Place a single knot in each individual strand and trim the ends. Using a thick sewing needle, push both ends of the braiding cord into the bead as well.

Easy Multicolored Bracelet

The simplest way to create a multicolored bracelet is to use variegated yarn; a striped pattern will appear as you're spinning—it's magic!

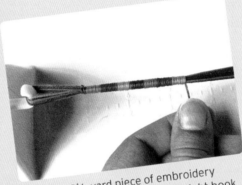

1. Cut an 8½-yard piece of embroidery thread and double knot it to the right hook of the spinning loom. Wrap 17 lengths around the hooks and create a 1-in.-long attachment loop on the left side of the loom. Note that the loop needs to be large enough for the bead to pass through. Start spinning, making sure to hold the thread close to the loom.

2. When the bracelet is about 7½ in. long, keep spinning back and forth over a ¼-in. length to make a thicker end and finish with a double-loop knot.

3. Cut your bracelet from the loom, close to the right hook. Slip all 18 threads though the wooden bead.

4. Divide the threads into 2 groups of 8 and double knot. Trim ends as needed.

Tip

Explore the yarn and embroidery aisles of your local craft store and experiment with making simple bracelets out of novelty yarns: variegated, dip-dyed, LUREX®, baker's twine, and so on. You'll be amazed with the results! Just stay away from the heavier, bulky yarns, which may not weave as nicely.

Color-Block Wrap Bracelet

If you don't have a spinning loom, you can achieve a similar result by simply wrapping embroidery floss around a rope core. What's more, there's no limit to how long, or how thick, you can make this wrap bracelet. Just make sure your end caps fit your choice of cord.

SKILL LEVEL
Beginner

CORD
Remnants of embroidery floss (each at least 25 in. long), in different colors

1½ yards of ¼-in.-dia. diamond braided polypropylene rope

NOTIONS
Scissors

2 end caps to fit the ¼-in.-dia. cord

Glue of your choice

2 jump rings

Pliers

Bracelet clasp

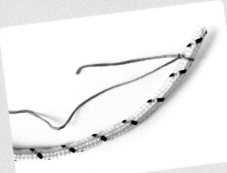

1. Start with a 25-in. length of embroidery floss and double knot it around the polypropylene rope about 1 in. from the end. Make sure the short end of the floss is about 2 in. longer than the intended length of the color block.

2. Wrap the longer end of the embroidery floss neatly and tightly around the polypropylene rope and over the short end of the floss. Wrapping over the short end left from your knot helps conceal the end and gives your piece a more streamlined look. When you have achieved the desired length of this first color block, tie both ends of the floss together with a double knot.

3. Repeat this process with the remaining colors in varying lengths, making sure that you wrap over the ends of the previous color.

4. When your wrap bracelet has the desired look and length, trim both ends of the rope core as close as possible to the floss, and insert into the end caps with a few drops of strong glue. Using pliers and jump rings, attach the end caps to the bracelet clasp. Let the glue dry for a few hours before use.

Tip

This is a great project to work through your leftover stash of embroidery floss. Experiment with the palette, layout, and pattern of the color blocks to create your very own look.

Crazy Zigzag Bracelet

No need to line up your yarn just so; it's the random wrapping and spinning along with the crazy color combinations that make this bracelet unique.

SKILL LEVEL
Intermediate

CORD
Four 3½-yard pieces of embroidery floss in different colors

NOTIONS
Scissors
Spinning loom

Tip
Bear in mind that the first color you loop with will be the least visible in your final bracelet and the last color will be the most visible.

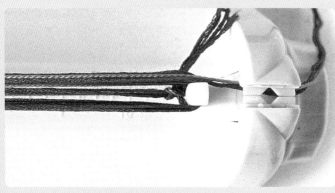

1. Double knot your 4 pieces of embroidery floss together to the right hook of the spinning loom. Wrap 5 lengths around the hooks and create a 1-in.-long attachment loop on the left side of the loom. Separate the first color you want to use and slip the other three through the gear slot on the right-hand side. Spin with the first thread, spacing it randomly. When your bracelet is about 7 in. long, finish with a double-loop knot.

2. *The most important step*: flip the loom around. Remove one of the three remaining colors from the gear slot and spin to the end of the bracelet *and back*, spacing it randomly. Finish with a double-loop knot.

3. Remove another color from the gear slot, spin randomly back and forth, and double-loop knot. Do the same with the last remaining color.

4. Cut your bracelet from the loom, making sure to cut as close as possible to the right hook. Separate the threads into two groups, making sure there are some looping threads in each half. Tie a single knot. The bracelet closes by putting half of the thread through the attachment loop and tying a tight double knot.

Crown Knot Bracelet

Everybody has fond memories of making lanyard bracelets like these in summer camp. Using satin cord and a pretty two-tone palette makes them just a little more versatile and fashionable.

SKILL LEVEL
Advanced

CORD
2 yards of 2 mm satin nylon cord (rattail) in Color A (dark)

2 yards of 2 mm satin nylon cord (rattail) in Color B (light)

NOTIONS
Scissors

1. Fold both 2-yard pieces over in the middle and tie a single knot, leaving a loop about ¾ in. long. Divide the 4 strands into 2 horizontal (one dark and one light color) and 2 vertical strands (one dark and one light color).

2. Make a 4-strand crown knot, as shown. To do this, place 1 strand behind your thumb. Beginning at this strand, move clockwise, laying each strand over the top of the strand in front of it. When you get to the strand before your thumb, remove your thumb and feed the strand through the hole left by your thumb. Tighten the knot well.

3. Repeat the process by folding the dark strand over the dark half of the knot and the opposite light strand over the light half of the knot in the opposite direction. Keep knotting until the knotted braid is about 5½ in. long.

4. Gather all 4 strands and tie into a firm single knot about ½ in. under the end of the braid, make a single knot in each individual strand, and trim the ends. Feed the end with the knots through the loop on the other end and tie.

Tip

You can keep the length of the crown knot braid fairly short; because it stretches, it will fit a variety of wrists.

Bulky Chain Bracelet

Give an existing, or newly made, chain bracelet a unique upgrade with a bundle of multicolored yarn and two festive tassels.

SKILL LEVEL
Beginner

CORD
Approx. 10 yards of embroidery floss, in different complementary colors

NOTIONS
Existing chain bracelet or 6 in. of ¼-in.-wide chain and lobster closure

Pliers

Scissors

Tip

You can personalize all kinds of chain jewelry using this technique: experiment with colors, placement of tassels, amount of floss, and weaving patterns.

1. Attach the lobster closure to the chain by opening and closing the last chain link with a pair of pliers. Cut 9 pieces of embroidery floss in different complementary colors ½ yard long (I used various reds and purples to keep the look consistent). Tie this bundle to one end of the bracelet, leaving 2-in.-long ends.

2. Weave the bundle of floss through the chain. Tie the ends to the last chain link with a single knot, as shown, and trim to 2 in. long.

3. Wrap a 2-yard piece of embroidery floss around 3 of your fingers and snip the wrapped embroidery floss to create a little bundle that will become part of the tassel. Split the ends of the floss hanging off the bracelet into 2 groups and tie around the middle of the tassel bundle.

4. Fold all the yarns of the tassel down, and use an extra piece of floss (about a ½-yard length) to wrap around the top of the tassel and double knot, as shown. Trim the tassel as needed. Repeat this process to make a tassel on the other end of the bracelet.

Ball Chain Bracelet

Who knew plumbing components make for wonderful, and affordable, jewelry supplies? The brass ball chain gives this wrap bracelet weight and sparkle.

SKILL LEVEL
Beginner

CORD
6 yards of embroidery floss

NOTIONS
Scissors or wire cutters (do not use your best fabric scissors to cut the ball chain)

42 in. of ball chain with closure

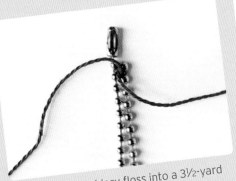

1. Cut the embroidery floss into a 3½-yard piece and a 2½-yard piece. Set aside the 2½-yard piece to finish the tassel later. Fold over both the ball chain and the 3½-yard piece in the middle. Tie the ends of the ball chain—so that one end has the closure attached—together with a double knot in the middle of the floss.

2. Gather both halves of the embroidery floss together and fold them over to the right, under the ball chain, and out in the middle between the 2 chains.

3. Fold both halves over to the left, under the ball chain, and out the middle between the 2 chains. Keep repeating this process until you reach the end of the chain. Separate both yarns, wrap them around the end of the chain, and double knot. Do not cut off the ends just yet.

4. Cut the 2½-yard length of embroidery floss into a 2-yard length and a ½-yard length. Wrap the 2-yard piece around 3 of your fingers and cut through the floss. Use the ends from Step 3 to tie this bundle in the middle to the end of the bracelet. Fold both sides of the bundle over and use the remaining length of floss to wrap over the top end of the tassel and secure with a double knot.

Tip

A 42-in. ball chain will make a bracelet that wraps 3 times around the wrist. Of course, you can make it longer or shorter as needed.

Twistie Earring Dangles

The twist technique results in a fun candy-cane look. Three short sections of loom work in alternating base colors are all you need to create some really traffic-stopping earrings.

SKILL LEVEL
Advanced

CORD
Three 6-yard pieces of embroidery floss in different colors

NOTIONS
Scissors

Spinning loom

Pair of earring wires with closed hook

Tip

As a variation on the twist technique, you can omit the step of looping a base color, and just twist directly over the core.

1. Cut each of the 3 different-colored 6-yard pieces of embroidery floss in half. Set one half of each color aside for the second earring. Double-knot 3 strands together to the right hook of the spinning loom. Wrap 5 lengths around the hooks and create a ½-in.-long attachment loop on the left side of the loom. Separate the base color you want to use, and slip the other two colors through the gear slot on the left-hand side. Spin with the first thread, making sure to hold it close to the loom. When the section is roughly 2¼ in. long, finish with a double-loop knot.

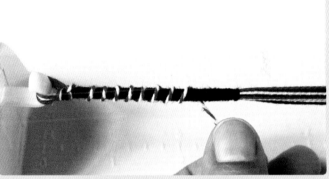

2. Take the 2 remaining colors out of the gear slot, and twist them onto themselves in the same direction that you are looping. Guide them into position as you are looping, spacing them equally. When you get to the end of the section, finish with a double-loop knot.

3. Measure the length of the remaining core thread. At one third of the remaining length, cut your section off of the loom, then remove the remaining 2 thirds from the loom by cutting as closely to the right hook as possible. Keep this bundle together. Separate the threads at the end of the section into two groups, making sure there are some looping threads in each half. Tie these around the middle of the bundle. Fold all threads down and trim to a 1-in. length.

4. Make the other 2 sections for the earring, each time using a different base color. The lengths of the other sections should be 2 in. and 1¾ in. Loop a small remnant through the hook of the earring wire and through the attachment loops of all three sections and make a tight double knot. Trim the ends. Repeat the entire process for the second earring.

Hex Nut Bracelet

The satin nylon cord used for this macramé bracelet interspersed with hex nuts is also known as rattail, an unfortunate term for such a great and versatile crafting cord.

SKILL LEVEL
Beginner

CORD
3 yards of 2 mm satin nylon cord (rattail)

NOTIONS
Scissors

16 small hex nuts (large enough to accommodate 2 strands of nylon cord)

Push pin

Foamcore or corkboard

1. Cut the piece of nylon cord in half. Gather up both lengths of cord and fold in half. Make a single knot about 1 in. from the end. Secure to the foamcore with a push pin.

2. Keep 2 strands in the middle. Tie the 2 outer strands into a half square knot, as shown.

3. Slip a hex nut onto the 2 middle strands and tie another half square knot as shown. Repeat these steps 15 more times.

4. Tie all 4 strands into a single firm knot about ½ in. below the end of the bracelet. Tie a single knot in each of the 4 ends at a length of 1½ in., and trim the ends below the knots.

Tip

As a variation, you can replace the hex nuts with beads of different shapes and sizes. Just make sure the bead holes are large enough to accommodate 2 strands of nylon cord.

Braided Bead Bracelet

This is one of the quickest projects in this book: a simple braided cord is transformed by inserting a dozen beads. This bracelet simply wraps and knots in place, so one size fits all!

SKILL LEVEL
Advanced

CORD
3 yards of waxed cotton cord

NOTIONS
Scissors
Push pin
Foamcore or corkboard
12 small beads

26

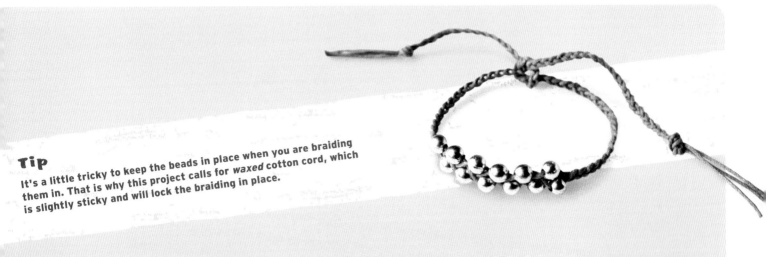

1. Cut 3 pieces of waxed cotton cord, each piece about 1 yard long, and knot them together about 1 in. from the end. You can secure the knot to foamcore with a push pin to keep your work in place. Braid the 3 cords until you have a length of about 20 in. To braid, spread out the 3 lengths out, put the left cord in the middle, then put the right cord in the middle. Keep repeating this process.

2. Slip 4 beads onto each cord and make a temporary knot at the bottom to prevent the beads from slipping off. Keep braiding, but push 1 bead to the top of the braid after each cord movement, as shown.

3. Keep doing this until you have braided all 12 beads into the body of the bracelet.

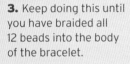

4. Undo the temporary knots at the end off the waxed cords and continue with a simple braid for another 20 in. Knot all 3 cords together and cut off, leaving a 1-in. length.

Color-Blocked Necklace

You can make more than just bracelets with your spinning loom. This wrapped necklace, which can be as long or short as you want it, is the perfect project to work through a big stash of embroidery floss. This necklace is made from 47 sections of loom work connected to each other.

SKILL LEVEL
Advanced

CORD
Each segment of the necklace calls for three 4-yard pieces of embroidery floss in different colors (the necklace shown has 47 segments)

NOTIONS
Scissors

Spinning loom

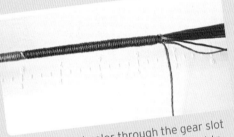

1. Double knot together 3 different-colored 4-yard pieces to the right hook of the spinning loom. Wrap 7 lengths around the hooks and create a ½-in.-long attachment loop on the left side of the loom. Separate the first color you want to use, and slip the other two through the gear slot on the right-hand side. Spin with the first thread, making sure to hold it close to the loom. When the section is roughly 2½ in. long, finish with a double-loop knot.

2. Slip the first color through the gear slot and take out the second color you want to use. Spin with the second thread, making sure to hold it close to the loom. You'll wind the second thread over the tail of your first thread. When the entire section is roughly 5 in. long, finish with a double-loop knot. Repeat this process with the third color, so that the total length of the section is now 7½ in.

3. Cut your section from the loom, making sure to cut as close as possible to the right hook. After making a whole bunch of similar sections in a variety of colors, attach them to one another by slipping the end threads of one section through the attachment loop of another. Using floss in a contrasting color, tie together with a tight double knot, leaving a 2-in. length.

4. Finally, wrap the long end of the remnant tightly over for about ¼ in. and tie together in a double knot. Once all pieces have been attached in one long loop, place the necklace around your neck, wrapping as desired.

Tip

There are many design variations possible with the color-blocking technique: You can experiment with the amount of color used or vary the length of the color blocks. And, of course, the necklace can be made with any of the other loom techniques as well.

Metric Equivalents

One inch equals approximately 2.54 centimeters. To convert inches to centimeters, multiply the figure in inches by 2.54 and round off to the nearest half centimeter, or use the chart below, whose figures are rounded off (1 centimeter equals 10 millimeters).

⅛ in.	=	3 mm	9 in.	= 23 cm
¼ in.	=	6 mm	10 in.	= 25.5 cm
⅜ in.	=	1 cm	12 in.	= 30.5 cm
½ in.	=	1.3 cm	14 in.	= 35.5 cm
⅝ in.	=	1.5 cm	15 in.	= 38 cm
¾ in.	=	2 cm	16 in.	= 40.5 cm
⅞ in.	=	2.2 cm	18 in.	= 45.5 cm
1 in.	=	2.5 cm	20 in.	= 51 cm
2 in.	=	5 cm	21 in.	= 53.5 cm
3 in.	=	7.5 cm	22 in.	= 56 cm
4 in.	=	10 cm	24 in.	= 61 cm
5 in.	=	12.5 cm	25 in.	= 63.5 cm
6 in.	=	15 cm	36 in.	= 92 cm
7 in.	=	18 cm	45 in.	= 114.5 cm
8 in.	=	20.5 cm	60 in.	= 152 cm

Resources

Michaels®
North America's largest specialty retailer of arts and crafts for the hobbyist.
www.michaels.com

Hobby Lobby®
Retailer for arts and crafts supplies, both online and with over 500 store locations.
www.hobbylobby.com

A.C. Moore
Arts and crafts superstores in the eastern United States from Maine to Florida.
www.acmoore.com

Hancock Fabrics
Craft and jewelry supplies.
www.hancockfabrics.com

Beverly's Fabric & Crafts
Craft and fabric store selling online and in retail shops throughout California.
www.beverlys.com

Jo-Ann Stores℠
Fabric and craft supplies.
www.joann.com

Herrschners®
Online resource for a wide variety of crafting supplies, including an impressive selection of embroidery floss.
www.herrschners.com

If you like these projects, you'll love these other fun craft booklets

Arm Knitting

Linda Zemba Burhance

EAN: 9781627108867

8½ × 10⅞, 32 pages

Product #078045, $9.95 U.S.

Fashionista Arm Knitting

Linda Zemba Burhance

EAN: 9781627109567

8½ × 10⅞, 32 pages

Product # 078050, $9.95 U.S.

Bungee Band Bracelets & More

Vera Vandenbosch

EAN: 9781627108898

8½ × 10⅞, 32 pages

Product # 078048, $9.95 U.S.

Mini Macramé

Vera Vandenbosch

EAN: 9781627109574

8½ × 10⅞, 32 pages

Product # 078049, $9.95 U.S.

DecoDen Bling

Alice Fisher

EAN: 9781627108874

8½ × 10⅞, 32 pages

Product # 078046, $9.95 U.S.

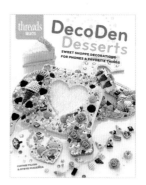

DecoDen Desserts,

Cathie Filian and Steve Piacenza

EAN: 9781627109703

8½ × 10⅞, 32 pages

Product # 078053, $9.95 U.S.

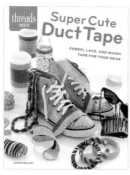

Super Cute Duct Tape

Jayna Maleri

EAN: 9781627109901

8½ × 10⅞, 32 page

Product # 078056, $9.95 U.S.

Rubber Band Charm Jewelry

Maggie Marron

EAN: 9781627108881

8½ × 10⅞, 32 page

Product # 078047, $9.95 U.S.

Beautiful Burlap

Alice Fisher

EAN: 9781627109888

8½ × 10⅞, 32 page

Product # 078054, $9.95 U.S.